Can a brave war dog save
the men in his marine unit?

On November 1, Jack and his handler, Private Gordon Wortman, were with a unit of marines deep in the jungle. Suddenly the unit was attacked by Japanese soldiers. Private Wortman was shot in the leg. Jack was shot in the back. It looked like the whole unit would be killed unless more marines came to their aid.

The unit leader had an idea. He wrote a message on a piece of paper and slipped it into a pouch on Jack's neck. "We're counting on you," Wortman told the dog.

Jack was so badly hurt that he could barely stay on his feet. But he knew he had a job to do. He ran into the jungle as Japanese soldiers fired machine guns after him. Wortman and the other men could only wait and hope.

TRUE TALES OF Courageous Dogs

Joanne Mattern

SCHOLASTIC INC.

New York Toronto London Auckland Sydney
Mexico City New Delhi Hong Kong Buenos Aires

ISBN-13: 978-0-439-02713-7
ISBN-10: 0-439-02713-6

12 11 10 9 8 7 6 5 4 3 2 1   7 8 9 10 11 12/0

Printed in the U.S.A.   40

This edition first printing, March 2007

TABLE OF CONTENTS

Introduction 7

Chapter 1
STUBBY: America's First Dog Hero 9

Chapter 2
CHIPS: World War II Hero 14

Chapter 3
ANDY: The Devil Dog 19

Chapter 4
CAESAR: Special Delivery 23

Chapter 5
JACK: Courage Under Fire 27

Chapter 6
NEMO: A Wounded Hero 30

Chapter 7
WOLF AND CHARLIE: A Perfect Team 35

Chapter 8
TORO: From Pet to Protector 39

Chapter 9
More Heroic War Dogs 42

Chapter 10
SAM: Danger on the Job 48

Chapter 11
ARON: The Ultimate Sacrifice   51

Chapter 12
ELWAY: Sniffing Out Drugs   53

Chapter 13
PACO: Patrolling the Border   57

Chapter 14
Bombs Away   60

Chapter 15
The Beagle Brigade   64

Chapter 16
KAZE: From Death Row to Saving Lives   67

Chapter 17
BRIDGET: Smelling a Survivor in the Snow   69

Chapter 18
DAKOTA: Changing People's Minds   72

Chapter 19
The Dogs of 9–11   77

Chapter 20
After the Shooting Stops   87

Chapter 21
Honoring Heroic Dogs   90

For More Information   93

INTRODUCTION

For hundreds of years, courageous men and women have protected our country and its citizens. Some of these brave people have marched into battle and fought enemy soldiers. Others have patrolled our streets and borders, or rushed to rescue injured or trapped victims of disasters. Many have been wounded, or even killed, doing their duty.

Men and women are not the only heroes who have worked to keep us safe, however. There are also four-legged heroes. These furry fighters are dogs.

Not every dog can go into battle or help police, the border patrol, and rescue workers. War dogs; police dogs; drug-, bomb-, and plant-and-food-sniffing dogs; and search-and-rescue dogs are specially chosen and trained. These dogs need to be alert, obedient, and eager to work. They are trained to respond to voice commands and hand signals. A war or police dog cannot be so aggressive that he attacks a person for no reason. However, he must be willing and able to defend himself and his handler from danger.

Every specially trained dog works with a human handler. The handler and the dog are a team. They attend classes to learn to work together. The dog must follow his handler's commands, even if they put him in danger. At the same time, the handler must trust his dog and respect his instincts. Usually, the dog lives with the handler and his family, even when the team is not on duty.

Dogs receive specialized training for particular jobs.

War dogs must be able to tolerate the sound of gunfire and explosions without getting scared. Search-and-rescue dogs are trained to respond to certain smells and sounds and to alert their handlers when they have found something. Likewise, dogs that sniff out drugs, bombs, or illegal plants and foods learn to identify the smell of the materials they are seeking, and to alert their handlers without disturbing the suspicious packages they have identified. Police dogs use their sharp senses to locate people. These dogs must get used to riding in cars and patrolling busy streets in cities and large towns.

Dogs have been protecting people in war and peace for thousands of years. Scientists have found pictures of war dogs in Assyrian temples and on Egyptian walls from as far back as 4000 B.C. Historical accounts describe how ancient Persians sent large packs of dogs into battle. When the ancient Romans invaded Great Britain two thousand years ago, the British used large dogs called mastiffs to fight against the Roman army. Other ancient leaders, such as Genghis Khan, brought dogs into battle with them.

During the Middle Ages, dogs wore small suits of armor and went into battle along with armed knights on horseback. These dogs often wore spiked collars and attacked the horses ridden by enemy soldiers. Other dogs did not actually fight in wars. Instead they served as guards or sentries to warn soldiers of danger.

The pages of this book contain many stories of dogs who became heroes in war and in peace. Come and meet Stubby, Chips, Wolf, Sam, Bridget, and more dog heroes.

STUBBY
America's First Dog Hero

For many years, dogs were not an official part of the United States Army. But that did not stop soldiers from bringing dogs into camp with them. Dogs were good company. They helped ease the loneliness of long, dark nights. With a dog nearby, many soldiers felt safer and not as frightened of battles and other dangers.

Dogs often became mascots, or special pets, that belonged to army units. One of these dogs was a stray pit bull named Stubby. Although Stubby was not specially trained to be a war dog, he became America's first dog hero during World War I.

Stubby began his life on the streets of Hartford, Connecticut. In 1916, a young man named Robert Conroy found Stubby and adopted him. Conroy was a corporal in the 102nd Infantry of the U.S. Army. He and his unit were training for combat at a camp near Hartford.

Although dogs were not allowed at the camp, Conroy smuggled Stubby in. Soon, Stubby became a friend to everyone in the 102nd Infantry.

In time, the 102nd was transferred to Newport News, Virginia, for final training before shipping out to fight the war in Europe. The soldiers wanted Stubby to come with them, even though it was against the rules. Conroy was traveling to Newport News in a vehicle loaded with supplies. He hid Stubby under the equipment and brought him along.

In late 1917, Conroy and his unit boarded a ship for France, where World War I was raging. The soldiers were not about to leave Stubby behind. So they pulled him through a porthole and onto the ship when no one was looking. When the 102nd Infantry landed in St. Nazaire, France, in January 1918, Stubby was with them.

The 102nd was sent into battle on February 5, 1918. Stubby didn't waste any time proving that he was a special dog. Soon after his arrival at the front lines, he was exposed to poisonous gas fired at the American troops by enemy German soldiers. Conroy rushed him to the closest field hospital for treatment, and fortunately, Stubby was soon able to return to his unit.

This exposure left Stubby highly sensitive to the smell of poison gas. Late one night, just a few weeks after the first attack, he knew something was wrong. He began barking loudly and woke up some of the soldiers. The men realized that the Germans had launched another gas attack. Stubby's early warning gave the troops time to put on their gas masks and protect themselves from the attack. Once he knew the men were safe, Stubby wisely left the area and didn't return until the air had cleared.

Another time, Stubby found a German soldier who had slipped into the camp. The dog attacked the spy and bit him on the backside. When Corporal Conroy heard Stubby barking, he rushed to capture the enemy soldier. Once again, Stubby had protected his human friends.

Because Stubby's hearing was much sharper than any human's, he often warned the soldiers when an enemy attack was near. The Americans soon learned that if Stubby lay on the ground and covered his head with his paws, it meant explosive shells were about to fall. Stubby's warning gave the soldiers time to take cover, and his actions saved lives.

One day, Stubby accidently walked into "no-man's-land," an area that was too close to enemy lines to be safe. He was injured by shrapnel from a grenade. After he recovered, the brave pit bull took part in many major battles with the 102nd. Along with alerting the soldiers to danger, he also delivered messages for the troops. Other times, Stubby just lay down near wounded soldiers to comfort them and keep them company until help arrived. The men of the 102nd were so proud of Stubby that they made a special Victory Medal and hung it on his collar.

Word of Stubby's heroic acts soon spread beyond the battlefield. A group of French women made a blanket to keep Stubby warm on chilly winter nights.

Soldiers pinned medals on the blanket. Soon, Stubby was known as the "Hero Dog."

Stubby served in the army for nineteen months and took part in seventeen battles. Finally, Robert Conroy's tour of duty was over, and Stubby accompanied his friend back home to America.

Stubby continued to be honored even after the war was over. In 1920, the Eastern Dog Club of Boston gave him a silver medal inscribed: "Awarded to the Hero Dog Stubby." In 1921, the Humane Society made a gold medal for Stubby and asked General John Joseph "Black Jack" Pershing, who had been a major commander of the American forces in World War I, to present it to the dog.

Stubby was also named an honorary sergeant by the U.S. Marines and became a lifetime member of the American Red Cross, the YMCA, and the American Legion. He toured the United States and appeared in many parades. He even met three U.S. presidents: Woodrow Wilson, Warren G. Harding, and Calvin Coolidge. This was one important dog!

Stubby finally died of old age in 1926, in the arms of his beloved friend Robert Conroy. But his story did not end there. The Red Cross Museum in Washington, D.C., asked to have Stubby's body to display it. A taxidermist (a person who prepares dead animals for exhibit) removed Stubby's skin. Then he made a plaster mold of Stubby's skeleton and stretched the dog's skin over it. Finally, Stubby was put on display. He was wearing the blanket made by the French women, and all his medals.

Stubby was exhibited for almost thirty years. Over time, some of his skin and fur wore away and he started to look shabby. People also lost interest in World War I and its hero dog. Finally, the Red Cross Museum gave Stubby to the Smithsonian Institution's Museum of Natural History. The museum's staff didn't quite know what to do with Stubby, so they packed him in a wooden box and put him in a storeroom. Later, he was sent to a National Guard Armory in Connecticut. He is still there today.

FAST FACT: Rin Tin Tin was a German shepherd who appeared in many popular movies during the 1920s. The puppy was originally the mascot of a German army unit. Rin Tin Tin came to the United States when American soldiers found him in a German trench after a battle.

CHIPS
World War II Hero

When the United States entered World War II, dogs finally became an official part of the American army. A group of breeders and owners formed an organization called Dogs for Defense. They convinced the army to use the dogs in the war effort. Then they asked the American people to send their dogs to war. More than forty thousand people donated their dogs to the war effort. These army dogs became known as the K-9 Corps.

FAST FACT: The K-9 Corps got its name because "K-9" sounds like "canine."

Becoming a part of the army was not easy. Dogs had to weigh between 55 and 85 pounds and be 23 to 28 inches tall at the shoulder. They also had to be between fourteen months and five years old. At first, any breed of dog was accepted. Later, the K-9 Corps limited enrollment to seven breeds: German shepherds, Doberman pinschers, Belgian sheepdogs, collies, Siberian huskies, malamutes, and Eskimo dogs. These breeds had the best personalities for war work and could be trained easily to respond to commands. Male dogs usually performed better than females, so most K-9 dogs were male.

Each dog that tried out for the K-9 Corps was given a complete physical examination and tested to make sure he or she could perform in combat. More than 75 percent of the dogs failed these examinations and were sent home. The rest were tattooed inside one ear with an ID number and sent to a special boot camp for fourteen weeks of training. Here they completed basic obedience training, ran obstacle courses, and learned to jump out of helicopters and planes. Many of the dogs were then sent overseas to fight alongside American soldiers. Other dogs stayed in the United States to patrol military bases, coastal communities, defense plants, and other places that might be attacked by the enemy.

One of the first dogs to be sent overseas was Chips. Chips was a mixed-breed dog—part German shepherd, part collie, and part husky. He belonged to Edward Wren of Pleasantville, New York. Wren had bought the dog in 1940 to be a companion and protector for his two young daughters.

Although Chips was gentle and playful with the Wren girls, he often attacked other dogs, cats, and people. Many of the neighbors complained about Chips. In 1942, Chips bit the garbageman. Edward Wren decided that the dog might be better off serving in the army instead of being a family pet. He donated Chips to Dogs for Defense.

Chips was sent to the Front Royal War Dog Center in Virginia for training. He did well and was matched with a handler, Private John Rowell. In October 1942, Rowell and Chips and their unit, the Thirtieth Infantry, left the United States for Morocco.

Chips, along with three other dogs in the Thirtieth Infantry, worked as a sentry. The dogs stayed with their handlers during the day and patrolled the edges of the camp at night to keep the soldiers safe. Chips was also part of the security force when U.S. president Franklin D. Roosevelt and British prime minister Winston Churchill met in Casablanca during the war.

In July 1943, the Thirtieth Infantry was sent to Sicily, an island off the coast of Italy. There they joined Brigadier General George S. Patton's Seventh Army. And there Chips would perform an amazing act of courage.

At 4:20 in the morning of July 10, several soldiers, including Rowell and Chips, landed on a beach in Sicily. They were walking along the shore when they saw a small hut. Rowell did not know it, but the hut was full of enemy Italian soldiers. Suddenly, these soldiers began shooting at Rowell and the other Americans.

Without warning, Chips pulled away from Rowell and rushed toward the hut with his leash trailing behind him. As the dog entered the hut, the gunfire stopped. Moments later an Italian soldier stumbled out of the hut. Chips was jumping around him, snarling and biting at his arms and throat. Three more soldiers followed with their arms raised in surrender.

When Rowell called Chips back to his side, he saw that the dog had powder burns and a small cut on his head. Obviously the Italians had fought hard. They had even tried to shoot Chips at close range. But the dog had proved to be too much for the Italian soldiers, who were quickly taken prisoner by the Americans.

Chips was not finished. Later that night, he began barking. When Rowell went to see what was happening, he found ten Italian soldiers walking down the road. Rowell took the enemy soldiers prisoner.

The events of July 10 made Chips a hero. Although it was against army rules to give medals to animals, several army officers decided to honor Chips. On September 9, 1943, Captain Edward Parr recommended Chips for the Distinguished Service Cross. On October 24, Chips was given the Silver Star. A few weeks later, he received the Purple Heart, which is given to all soldiers wounded in battle.

Chips became a star in the United States. Many newspapers described his heroic actions. Politicians gave speeches about him.

Unfortunately, all the attention Chips was receiving got him into trouble. William Thomas was the national commander of the Military Order of the Purple Heart. He wrote a letter to President Franklin D. Roosevelt, complaining that giving the Purple Heart to a dog was an insult to the many men who had received the award. Thomas said that he appreciated the heroic work of Chips and the other dogs, but that they should have their own medal to honor them.

In February 1944, Major General J. A. Ulio answered Thomas's letter. He said that the army did not allow medals to be given to animals and that heroic dogs would not be honored that way anymore. All of Chips' awards were taken away and his medals had to be returned. Even though he did not get to keep them, Chips was the only dog ever to receive official medals from the U.S. Army.

However, John Rowell and the other soldiers who worked with Chips did not care what the government said. The Thirtieth Infantry was fighting in Italy, and Chips was still an important part of the unit. The men had their own ceremony for Chips and gave him the medals they had earned.

By December 1943, Chips was tired and nervous from the constant gunfire and the stress of battle. He was transferred to a position in France, away from enemy lines. Later, Chips worked as a sentry at a prisoner-of-war camp. Finally, on October 20, 1945, Chips came home to the United States. After a short stay at Front Royal, he went back to live with his original owner, Edward Wren, on December 10.

Sadly, Chips was in poor health by the time he got home. He died just a few months later, on April 12, 1946.

FAST FACT: War dogs are trained to allow only their handlers to touch them. In 1943, Chips met General Dwight Eisenhower, who later became president of the United States. When Eisenhower tried to pet the dog, Chips bit his hand!

3

ANDY
The Devil Dog

In 1943, a very special group of 12,524 soldiers and 24 dogs arrived on Bougainville Island in the South Pacific. The dogs were part of a unit known as the First Marine Dog Platoon. Called "devil dogs" after the nickname given to the U.S. Marines by German soldiers during the First World War, they were specially trained to fight with the marines against the Japanese army in World War II.

One of these dogs who came to Bougainville was a big black Doberman pinscher named Andy. Andy may have been a "devil dog," but he was an angel to the many men whose lives he saved.

FAST FACT: The marines promoted their dogs after the animals had been in service for a certain length of time. If a dog served long enough, he could outrank his handler!

The tropical islands of the Pacific were a difficult place to live and fight. Soldiers and their dogs lived in snake-infested swamps. The air was thick with mosquitoes and other insects. The hot, wet climate caused dangerous infections. Many soldiers became sick with malaria and other tropical diseases. The thick jungle was the perfect hiding place for snipers and enemy soldiers.

Most of the marines' dogs wore leashes as they patrolled the jungles with their handlers. Andy was so well trained, however, that he could work off-leash. On November 1, 1943, Andy led his handler, Private Robert Lansley, and 250 other soldiers down a narrow, rough trail. Andy trotted up the trail, about 25 yards ahead of Lansley and the other men.

At first, it seemed as if Andy were enjoying a walk in the jungle. Suddenly he stopped and growled. Lansley saw the hairs on the back of the dog's neck stand straight up. He knew Andy's terrific senses of hearing and smell had detected enemy soldiers hiding in the woods, waiting to ambush the Americans.

Lansley and the other men dropped to the ground just seconds before enemy bullets whizzed over their heads. If Andy had not warned them, the men would have been killed.

That was not the only time Andy saved the men. He alerted them to ambushes three times that day. Each time, Lansley and the other marines were able to take cover before the bullets started flying. Eventually they found the enemy soldiers and defeated them. That day,

Andy and his company covered more ground than any other group of marines. Even more remarkable, not one marine was injured or killed during the march.

Two weeks after the marines arrived on Bougainville, Andy led Lansley and another marine, Private Jack Mahoney, into the jungle. Their job was to find a hidden outpost where Japanese soldiers were firing machine guns at American troops. Because of the deadly gunfire, the troops could not move forward.

Lansley usually had no trouble figuring out when Andy had sensed danger. The dog would stop moving. Then he would point his head in the direction of the danger. That day, however, Lansley noticed that Andy was behaving strangely. As they walked through the jungle, Andy froze. First he pointed to the left. Then he turned and pointed to the right. Was something confusing the dog?

Lansley had faith in his partner. He knew Andy was trying to tell him something. The soldier lay down on the ground and crawled up next to his dog. He looked through the thick leaves and saw a banyan tree in front of him. Everything seemed normal at first. Then Lansley noticed that there were two bushes next to the banyan tree, one on the left of the tree and the other on the right. Something about those bushes did not look normal.

Suddenly Lansley understood what Andy was trying to tell him. Those bushes had not grown there naturally. Instead, they had been placed there to hide something. That something was two machine-gun nests. Andy had been pointing to the left and the right because there were *two* machine guns, not just one.

Lansley acted quickly. He fired into the bushes, then threw grenades into the leaves to destroy the nests. At last, the American soldiers could march farther onto the island.

FAST FACT: Many reports about units that used war dogs included the same sentence: "No patrols led by dogs were fired on first or suffered casualties."

CAESAR
Special Delivery

Irving, Morris, and Max Glazer were brothers who lived in the Bronx, New York. The three teenagers wanted a dog more than anything. Once they had saved sixty dollars, they went looking for a pet.

After searching for three months, the Glazers found a nine-week-old black-and-gray German shepherd puppy named Caesar von Steuben. He was the best-looking dog they had seen, so they bought him.

Irving became especially close to Caesar. He taught the dog many tricks, including how to sit up, shake hands, stay, and fetch a ball. But Caesar's favorite trick was delivering packages. Every day, Mrs. Glazer would send one of her sons to buy groceries. After he made the purchase, the boy would give the package to Caesar and tell him to take it home. Caesar always did exactly as he was told.

When the United States entered World War II in 1941, the three Glazer brothers enlisted in the armed forces to serve their country. Although Caesar was a beautiful, well-trained dog, he was too much work for Mr. and Mrs. Glazer to cope with by themselves. They thought about selling the dog, but they knew their sons would not like that idea. Then they heard that Dogs for Defense was asking for dogs to help in the war effort. They quickly volunteered Caesar for service.

Caesar was accepted and trained as a messenger. On October 4, 1943, he was sent to Bougainville Island in the South Pacific as part of the First Marine Dog Platoon. He had two handlers, Private Rufus Mayo and Private John Kleeman.

When the platoon arrived on Bougainville, it hurried into the jungle to set up a command post. But the marines had a big problem. There was no way to communicate with other soldiers. Telephone lines had been cut by enemy troops, and walkie-talkies could not send or receive messages through the thick jungle.

Caesar was the answer to the marines' problem. He spent three days bringing messages back and forth between the command post and soldiers fighting the Japanese army. Caesar did his job faithfully, even though enemy soldiers shot at him and grenades exploded all around him.

On their second night in the jungle, Private Mayo and Caesar were standing watch in a foxhole a few yards away from the rest of the company. Their job was to listen for an enemy attack and warn the other marines.

Although Mayo was listening carefully, he did not hear any strange noises that night. But Caesar did. He became restless and excited. Mayo listened even more closely. Suddenly he heard a grenade land right at his feet!

Mayo reached down, grabbed the grenade, and threw it back into the woods. It exploded. The next morning, Mayo found eight enemy soldiers who had been killed by the grenade. If it had not been for Caesar's warning, Mayo and the brave dog would have been the ones who died.

The next day, Caesar finished his ninth run as a messenger. Then something terrible happened. That night, some Japanese soldiers tried to attack the camp. Caesar ran away from Mayo to chase the soldiers. Mayo called Caesar back, but the enemy soldiers shot the dog twice as he turned around.

The marines fired back at the Japanese soldiers. Finally the shooting stopped. But Caesar was nowhere to be found. Mayo searched the camp and the surrounding jungle. He asked everyone if they had seen the dog, but no one had. What had happened to Caesar?

Then Mayo saw a trail of blood on the ground. He followed it to the command post nearby. He found Caesar lying in the bushes, badly hurt.

The marines rushed into action. They cut down some branches to use as poles and tied a blanket to them to make a stretcher. Then they lifted Caesar onto it. Twelve marines carried the stretcher to the hospital.

The rest of the unit lined up and saluted Caesar as he went past.

A little while later, a doctor came out to talk to Mayo and Kleeman. He told the men that he had been able to remove only one of the two bullets in Caesar's body. He thought the dog would recover, however.

The marines smothered Caesar with attention during his recovery. Soon the German shepherd was feeling much better. Three weeks later, he returned to the unit and his job as a sentry and messenger.

FAST FACT: When a man served his country during World War II, his family received a red, white, and blue star to put in their window. Families that donated dogs to the war effort received a red, white, and blue pawprint.

5
JACK
Courage Under Fire

Jack was another one of the "devil dogs" who served with the marines in the South Pacific during World War II. This Belgian shepherd started his life in a town near New York City. He belonged to a man who was drafted into the army. Jack's owner had no one to care for the dog, so he brought him to an animal shelter. Soon after, Jack was adopted by Joseph Verhaeghe and his son, Bobby.

Jack was a wonderful companion for Bobby and the rest of the Verhaeghe family. But when the United States entered World War II, Jack's life changed forever. Joseph Verhaeghe could not enlist in the army because of a medical condition. Still, he wanted to do something to help his country. When he heard about Dogs for Defense, he asked his wife and son to donate Jack to the cause.

Giving up Jack was a hard decision for young Bobby Verhaeghe to make. But he knew Jack could save the lives of American soldiers. Finally Bobby agreed, and Jack was sent into battle.

Like many other marine dogs, Jack took part in the invasion of Bougainville Island in the South Pacific. On November 1, 1943, Jack and his handler, Private Gordon Wortman, were with a unit of marines guarding a roadblock deep in the jungle. Suddenly the unit was attacked by a group of Japanese soldiers. Private Wortman was shot in the leg. Jack was shot in the back.

It looked like the whole unit would be killed unless more marines came to their aid. But how could they send for help? The Japanese had cut the only phone line linking the roadblock to headquarters. The marines were on their own.

Then the unit's leader had an idea. He crawled over to Wortman and Jack and asked the wounded soldier if he thought Jack could make it back to headquarters. Wortman said he thought Jack could, because Jack had "lots of guts."

The unit leader wrote a message on a piece of paper. Wortman slipped the message into a pouch on Jack's neck. "We're counting on you," Wortman told the dog. "Report to Paul." Paul was Jack's other handler, Private Paul Castracane, who was stationed at headquarters.

Jack was hurt so badly that he could barely stay on his feet. But he knew he had a job to do. He ran into the jungle as Japanese soldiers fired machine guns after him. Wortman and the other men could only wait and hope.

Despite his injury, Jack made it back to headquarters. Once he got there, he collapsed at Paul Castracane's feet. The soldier took the message and gave it to his commanding officer. Then he raced to the hospital with Jack.

Jack's courageous actions saved the day. Marine reinforcements rushed to the roadblock and defeated the Japanese soldiers. Wortman and the other injured Americans were taken to the hospital. Wortman recovered, and so did Jack. The marine platoon owed their lives to one brave dog.

FAST FACT: Many former owners wrote letters and sent money and gifts to dogs they had donated to the war effort.

NEMO
A Wounded Hero

When the United States became involved in the Vietnam War during the 1960s, war dogs were once again an important part of the military effort. About four thousand dogs worked with American troops.

Almost every branch of the armed forces used dogs. The air force and the army used dogs as sentries to protect Americans from enemy Viet Cong soldiers. The army also used dogs as scouts, and so did the marines.

German shepherds were the most common breed of war dog. Their high intelligence and ability to adapt to new situations made them a good choice for scouting and sentry work.

Labrador retrievers were especially valued as trackers. Their extraordinary sense of smell—up to one thousand times stronger than a person's—could locate enemy soldiers before they could fire on American units. The retrievers could also find injured or missing soldiers and pilots whose planes had crashed. Other breeds of dogs were specially trained to find enemy soldiers who tried to invade American camps by swimming underwater.

It soon became clear that soldiers were rarely injured or killed if a dog was nearby to protect them and warn the troops of danger. One report estimated that death rates fell by 65 percent in units that used dogs.

It did not take long for a close bond to develop between a dog and his handler. Soldiers often spoke of the unfailing love between man and animal. Some even felt closer to their dogs than they did to their own family. Tom Mitchell, who worked as a dog handler in Vietnam, told *Parade* magazine, "When we were sick, they would comfort us, and when we were injured, they protected us. They didn't care how much money we had or what color our skin was. Heck, they didn't even care if we were good soldiers. They loved us unconditionally. And we loved them. Still do."

It was not unusual for a war dog to protect his handler, even if doing so put the dog in danger. One dog who did just that was a German shepherd named Nemo.

Nemo was a two-year-old black-and-tan dog who belonged to an air force sergeant. In 1964, the air force bought the dog from his owner and trained him for war work at Lackland Air Force Base in San Antonio, Texas.

In January 1966, Nemo went to Vietnam as a sentry

with the 377th Air Police Squadron. Nemo and his handler patrolled the area at night, looking for enemy soldiers who might be trying to break into the Americans' camp.

On December 5, 1966, Nemo and his handler, Airman Second Class Robert Thorneburg, were patrolling an old cemetery near the American air base. Thorneburg was worried and sad. The night before, the 377th had fought with two groups of Viet Cong soldiers. Three Americans and their dogs had died in the battle. As he patrolled the cemetery, Thorneburg wondered if more enemy soldiers were hiding behind the shadowy gravestones or in the long, tangled grass.

When Thorneburg looked down at Nemo, he knew his fears were accurate. The dog's eyes were bright and alert, and his ears were standing straight up. The fur on his neck bristled. Thorneburg reached for his radio to call back to base and tell his unit that he was in danger.

Thorneburg never had a chance to make that call. A Viet Cong soldier fired at him, and the bullet struck the American in the shoulder. Another bullet hit Nemo in the face, cutting him open from his eye to his mouth.

As Thorneburg fell to the ground, four Viet Cong soldiers rushed out, waving their guns. Thorneburg thought he was going to be killed. But Nemo had other ideas. The dog attacked the four soldiers, even though he was bleeding heavily and his right eye was hanging out of its socket.

Nemo's attack gave Thorneburg a chance to call for help and fire his own gun at the enemy. A few minutes later, American troops came to the rescue. They found a very surprising sight.

Thorneburg lay on the ground, unconscious and bleeding. Nemo stood over him, protecting his injured master from any more harm. Two Viet Cong soldiers lay dead nearby. Both had severe dog bites, and one had been shot. The rescuers also found four abandoned machine guns in the grass. It was clear that the other Viet Cong soldiers had run away when they saw Nemo attack their comrades.

Thorneburg and Nemo were rushed back to the hospital at the air base. Nemo underwent emergency surgery to repair his injured face. His right eye had to be removed and he had a long scar where the bullet had ripped open his cheek, but he survived. Thorneburg was sent to an American hospital in Japan, where he also recovered from his wounds.

Nemo returned to active duty a few weeks after the attack. However, his wounds had not healed properly, so the air force decided to send him back to Lackland Air Force Base in Texas. By then, Nemo was a hero to people in the United States. He even received get-well cards from many children who had read about his brave deeds in the newspapers.

Nemo flew home and arrived at Lackland Air Force Base on July 22, 1967. A welcoming committee cheered as Nemo walked off the plane. Captain Robert M. Sullivan, who was in charge of the dog-training program at Lackland, said that Nemo "shows how valuable a dog is to his handler in staying alive."

Nemo received the best possible medical care at Lackland and soon recovered completely. Then he retired and lived comfortably at the base until he died in 1973. A sign near his kennel described Nemo's heroic actions and told everyone how special the bond between a dog and his handler could be.

FAST FACT: During the Vietnam War, 263 handlers and about 500 dogs were killed in battle.

WOLF AND CHARLIE
A Perfect Team

The American army's war dogs were so feared by the Viet Cong that they had orders to shoot the dogs first and the soldiers later. They were also given a special reward if they could prove that they had killed a dog or its handler. The enemy soldiers knew that an attack on Americans would be more successful without dogs there for protection.

Wolf was a black-and-gray German shepherd with big bat ears. He was trained as a scout and found many enemy traps during the three years he served in Vietnam. The dog was especially good at finding trip wires, which were wires stretched across a path and attached to a mine. If a person walked into a trip wire or even touched it, the wire would set off an explosion that could kill anyone nearby.

Wolf was stationed with the Forty-eighth Scout

Dog Platoon in Chu Lai, Vietnam. He had been there for a year before a young man named Charlie Cargo arrived in 1970. Soon Cargo and Wolf became a team. Their job was to lead patrols through the jungle and find safe routes for the army to follow.

Cargo often wrote about Wolf in letters home to his mother and five brothers and sister. Cargo's mother enjoyed the stories and never failed to include a box of dog biscuits in the packages she sent to her son.

Even though Wolf was a great dog, at first Cargo did not always believe what Wolf was telling him. That all changed not long after the two began working together. Cargo and Wolf were leading a group of soldiers up a hill covered with dirt and a few clumps of weeds. They were almost at the top when Wolf suddenly sat down and refused to move.

Cargo was annoyed at the delay. He was nervous because there was nowhere for the soldiers to hide if the enemy was close by. All he wanted to do was keep going and get to some cover. Cargo told the dog to move, but Wolf would not budge.

Maybe Wolf was thirsty, Cargo thought. He poured some water from his canteen into a tin cup and held it to the dog's mouth. Wolf ignored it.

Cargo looked at the few patches of weeds and shook his head. Surely if something was wrong, he would be able to see it. "You aren't sniffing the air or listening to anything," Cargo told the dog. "Stop worrying and let's go. Everything's okay."

When Wolf continued to sit there, Cargo's patience

snapped. He started to step around the dog. Suddenly Wolf moved sideways, blocking the young man's path. When Cargo started to move forward again, Wolf did an astonishing thing. He grabbed Cargo's hand between his powerful jaws and bit him.

Cargo was stunned. Waves of pain shot up his arm as blood ran down his hand. After a few moments, Wolf let go. Cargo checked the ground, knowing that something had to be very wrong for Wolf to turn against him. Then he saw something in the grass. It was a trip wire as thin as a single hair. The wire was only 2 feet in front of him. If Cargo had taken another step, he and Wolf would have been blown to pieces, along with at least ten other soldiers in the platoon.

Wolf and Cargo worked together for eleven months. During that time, Wolf led hundreds of soldiers through the jungle and other dangerous areas. One day, he was leading Cargo and the other men across a rice paddy. Suddenly Wolf stopped. Then he ran back to Cargo. There was something dangerous on the ground ahead. Another soldier went to investigate and found a booby trap that could have killed the entire unit. "Wolf was a lifesaver," Cargo said.

At one point, Cargo was promoted to sergeant. He was very excited, until he realized the promotion meant that he would not be able to work with Wolf anymore. Cargo decided his relationship with Wolf was more important than his rank. One day, he talked back to one of his superior officers. He knew that his punishment would be a demotion back to corporal. Now he could continue working with Wolf.

In 1971, Cargo's tour of duty in Vietnam was over. It was time for him to go home. But Cargo did not want to leave Wolf behind. He begged the military to discharge Wolf and let the dog go home with him. Cargo's family also tried to help, making phone calls to important military officers. Cargo even asked to stay in Vietnam for another tour of duty. But the military refused. Cargo went home, and Wolf stayed behind.

Cargo called December 7, 1971, "the worst day of my life." That was the day when he brought Wolf to the dog center and left him there. "I will never forget the confusion on his face when I walked away forever."

For thirty years, Cargo tried to find out what happened to Wolf. There was no proof, but Cargo suspected that the dog had been left behind in Vietnam when American troops withdrew from the country in 1975.

Then, in 2001, Cargo found some documents that told a surprising story. Wolf had returned to the United States in March 1972! He had been at Lackland Air Force Base in Texas until 1979, when he died of cancer.

Cargo wished that he had known Wolf was in Texas, so he could have visited him, or even brought the dog home before he died. Wolf's death ended the story of their partnership, but memories of their time together will live forever in Charlie Cargo's mind.

TORO
From Pet to Protector

When the United States entered the war in Vietnam, it did not take long for the demand for dogs to become greater than the supply. As they had done in World War II, the government asked the American people to donate their dogs for war duty. One woman who answered this call was Judy Dale of Canoga Park, California.

Judy and her husband, Arvin, had a lively German shepherd named Toro. When Judy heard about the need for war dogs, she knew Toro would be perfect. The dog was energetic and smart, and he loved to work. After talking it over, the Dales gave Toro to the U.S. Army.

Toro was accepted into the war dog program and sent to Fort Benning, Georgia, for training. There, he was matched with his handler, Specialist Carl Dobbins.

At first, the young man from North Carolina and the dog from California did not get along very well. Dobbins just couldn't get close to his new partner. Then, one day, Toro got a birthday letter from Judy and Arvin Dale. As Dobbins read the affectionate letter to Toro, he realized that the dog had been precious to his owners. Suddenly Dobbins was also able to see the special qualities in his dog. From then on, Dobbins and Toro were inseparable.

In September 1966, Toro would prove just how special he was. After they had completed their training, Dobbins and Toro were sent to Vietnam. One day, the two were asked to find a sniper who was hiding in the jungle. This sniper was firing on a platoon. The soldiers were unable to move because of the sniper's deadly aim.

Dobbins knew that he and Toro had only one chance to locate the sniper. If the sniper saw or heard them first, he would shoot them. Dobbins knelt down beside his dog. "Search," he told Toro, over and over. The big dog looked around. As he focused on one stand of trees, his body became alert.

Dobbins signaled to the soldiers that Toro had found something. Then he pointed to the place that the dog was watching intently. The soldiers opened fire and killed the sniper.

Dobbins was amazed at Toro's ability to find his target. Dobbins had no idea the sniper was hidden in the trees, and he hadn't even seen him until the enemy soldier was hit. He figured that at least ten more soldiers would have been killed if they had tried to find the sniper without Toro's help.

Toro and Dobbins worked together until Dobbins completed his tour of duty a year later. When Dobbins returned to the United States, Toro stayed behind and was paired with another handler. For Dobbins, coming home was a bittersweet experience, because he hated to leave Toro behind.

Although Dobbins never saw Toro again, he will always remember the spirited dog. "Without Toro, there's no way I would have made it back to the States," he later said. It was a feeling almost every dog handler echoed.

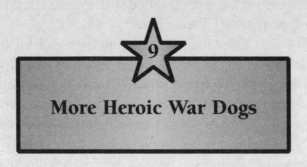

More Heroic War Dogs

There are many more stories to tell about canine heroes in combat. Here are just a few:

BOY

Boy was a scout dog who served with the marines on Japanese-held islands in the Pacific Ocean during World War II. One day, Boy started to alert his handler that there were enemy soldiers nearby. But the dog's warning came too late. The Japanese began shooting at the Americans.

Even though bullets were flying, Boy pulled away from his handler and ran right at the Japanese guns. As he ran, Boy was shot in the left shoulder. But his attack surprised the Japanese and gave the marines enough time to capture them and their weapons. After the battle, Boy's injury was treated, and he recovered.

WOLF

During World War II, Wolf was leading a patrol on Luzon Island in the Philippines when he sensed Japanese soldiers about 150 yards away. His warning gave the American soldiers enough time to take cover before the enemy attacked.

During the fighting, Wolf was shot several times. None of the men knew Wolf had been hurt, however, because the dog did not bark or show any signs of pain. Instead, he led the patrol to safety by alerting them to Japanese soldiers as the Americans made their way through enemy territory and back to camp. Not a single American soldier was killed.

When the patrol realized Wolf was injured, they rushed him to the hospital. But doctors were unable to save the brave dog. The official report of the incident says that Wolf "died of wounds received in action."

PEEFKE

Peefke was a scout dog in the Italian Alps during World War II. He saved countless lives by warning American soldiers when the enemy was near. One day, he discovered a trip wire attached to three mines. If they had gone off, every man in the patrol might have been killed.

Sadly, although Peefke saved many lives, he lost his own. The dog was killed in action by a hand grenade on March 20, 1945.

PRINCE

Prince was a German shepherd who spent his whole life in the war dog program. He died on October 2, 1968, at the War Dog Hospital in Long Binh, Vietnam. Long after Prince's death, his handler, Robert Ott, said, "I have remembered him every day for the last thirty-nine years and will continue to do so until I join him."

BRUISER

Bruiser was another German shepherd who served in Vietnam. In September 1969, Bruiser and his handler, John Flannelly, were leading a patrol near Da Nang. Suddenly the dog's ears went up. Seconds later, gunfire broke out. Flannelly was hit in the chest and fell to the ground.

Flannelly was sure he was going to die. With his last bit of strength, he told Bruiser to run to safety. But the dog stayed with him, staring sadly at his injured handler. Then Bruiser grabbed Flannelly's shirt in his teeth and began to pull. Flannelly held on to Bruiser's harness, and the dog pulled his handler to safety. As he did so, Bruiser was hit twice by gunfire.

Flannelly was seriously injured and needed to be transferred to another hospital for treatment. But he refused to go until he could see Bruiser. A soldier went to find the dog, and soon Bruiser crawled onto his bed and laid his head on Flannelly's face. "I was so happy to see him, I just hugged him and cried," Flannelly later recalled.

Flannelly recovered and returned to the United States, but he never found out what happened to Bruiser after he left Vietnam. "His loyalty was immeasurable," Flannelly said of his dog and partner.

"I'll never be able to thank him enough. I owe my life to that dog."

CARLO

During the Persian Gulf War of 1991, a Belgian Malinois named Carlo saved the lives of countless American soldiers. Carlo was trained to sniff out explosives. Working with Staff Sergeant Christopher Batta, Carlo found 167 concealed explosives in just two months. He averaged three finds a day!

Perhaps Carlo's most impressive discovery came when he started barking at a case of food meant for American soldiers. At first, Sergeant Batta thought Carlo was just hungry. But when he investigated, he found a bomb under the packages. If it had exploded, it would have killed many Americans.

Carlo saved the lives of ordinary citizens as well. One day, he sniffed out a huge group of explosives that had been hidden in a skyscraper in Kuwait by Iraqi soldiers. Several times, Carlo found bombs buried in neighborhoods where children played.

On October 10, 1991, Sergeant Batta received the Bronze Star for his service in Kuwait. Although he was proud of the award, Batta felt Carlo deserved it more than he did. After the ceremony, Batta took off the medal and pinned it on Carlo's collar. "Carlo worked harder than me," he said. "He was always in front of me."

FAST FACT: Dogs are the only soldiers who do not wear dog tags.

TRIPOD AND THE DOGS OF BOSNIA

Tripod was an ordinary stray dog who lived in the war-torn city of Srebrenica, Bosnia. The most unusual thing about her was that she had only three legs. Tripod may have been injured in the fighting between different ethnic groups that tore apart Bosnia, beginning in the late 1990s. But she was more than just a dog to the American troops stationed in the area. And Tripod started a canine tradition that is still saving lives today.

No one is sure where Tripod came from. One day, an American soldier made friends with the three-legged dog by giving her a few bites of ham. The hungry dog never forgot this act of kindness. From that day on, she stayed with the soldier, providing company and security.

Later, Tripod had puppies. As soon as they were old enough, Tripod brought the puppies to meet the American soldier and his friends. Soon, the younger dogs also became attached to the American troops.

Tripod is no longer alive, but the tradition she started continues. As the U.S. peacekeeping forces do their job in Bosnia, they are constantly accompanied by stray dogs. These dogs are more than just good company. As soon as the Americans ride into town in their armored vehicles, the dogs run barking into the road to escort them through Srebrenica's streets. "The other soldiers told us about these dogs when we were training, and I didn't believe them," said Staff Sergeant Joe Jimmerson. "And the first time we rolled into town, sure enough, they're here."

As they travel with the Americans, the dogs dart into alleys and side streets to check for danger. And there is plenty of danger is Srebrenica, everything from snipers to unexploded bombs.

When the soldiers patrol on foot, the dogs go with them. If anyone suspicious approaches a soldier, the dogs go on guard, snapping and growling at the person until the soldier can make sure the stranger is not a threat.

The American soldiers love their canine companions. "They're our friends," said Private First Class Rena Exler.

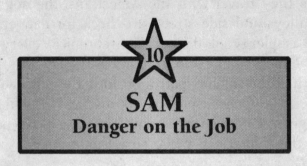

10
SAM
Danger on the Job

War dogs are not the only canines sworn to serve and protect Americans. Every day, in cities and towns across the United States, specially trained police dogs work with officers to capture criminals, find victims, and keep people safe. These dogs never hesitate to act—even if it means putting their own lives in danger.

Sam was the perfect example of such bravery. The six-year-old German shepherd worked for the Minneapolis police department, along with his handler, Officer Andy Stender.

On March 3, 2000, Sam and Stender were called into a very dangerous situation. A man was barricaded inside his house with a butcher knife. He threatened to use it against anyone who came near him, including the police.

Officers talked to the man for several hours, but he still would not come out peacefully. Finally the police fired chemicals into the house. These chemicals would make the man sick. The police hoped that he would run out of the house to get away from the gas, or that he would feel so sick that he would not be able to hurt anyone who went inside.

The officers waited a few minutes for the gas to take effect. Then Officer Stender sent Sam inside the house to find the man. Without hesitating, Sam ran to do his job.

He found the man right away. He dragged him outside, where the police were waiting. Suddenly the man lunged at Sam and stabbed him in the neck.

Sam did not let his injury stop him. He kept pulling the man to the police officers. But when Stender saw the blood running down his partner's fur, he called Sam off. As police finally captured the man, Sam was rushed to the hospital.

Doctors at the University of Minnesota Small Animals Hospital worked hard to save Sam's life. He had lost so much blood that his heart actually stopped during emergency surgery. Luckily, the doctors were able to revive him. At last, Sam was out of danger.

Unfortunately, the knife wound had damaged nerves in Sam's neck. Although he recovered from his injury, he was unable to do police work anymore. Instead, Sam became Officer Stender's pet.

Many people in Minneapolis were proud of Sam's heroic efforts. So was the police department. A few months after the incident, the police recommended that Sam receive a special medal of honor. "He was a highly thought of dog, and the officers thoroughly enjoyed working with him," said a police department spokeswoman. But if Sam could talk, he would probably say that he was just doing his job.

ARON
The Ultimate Sacrifice

Police dogs are often exposed to danger as they work to keep our communities safe. Sometimes these dogs pay for their dedication with their lives. That's what happened to Aron, a K-9 dog who was a member of the Nashville, Tennessee, police department.

On May 14, 1998, Officer Terry Burnett and his K-9 partner, Aron, received an urgent call. A man carrying a gun had just robbed a bank. When police arrived on the scene, the gunman fled into the woods. Officer Burnett and Aron followed him.

Aron used his sharp sense of smell to track the robber. It did not take long for the dog to find the man. When Aron cornered him, the robber opened fire with two semiautomatic handguns. Officer Burnett was struck in the foot. Aron rushed to stand between his handler and the gunman to protect Burnett from being injured again. The man shot Aron several times as other officers raced in to pull Burnett to safety.

Even though he was injured, Aron kept working. He followed Officer Burnett so he could continue to protect him. Aron had to drag himself backward on his hind legs, because his front legs had been so badly injured by the gunfire. Then he lay down on top of Officer Burnett to shield him from any further harm.

Another K-9 dog and handler moved toward the suspect. When the gunman fired at them, he was shot and killed by a Special Weapons and Tactics (SWAT) team also at the scene.

Officers tried to convince Burnett to go to the hospital for treatment. But the policeman refused. He knew that Aron needed help more urgently than he did. Aron was rushed to an emergency animal clinic, but it was too late. The dog died from his injuries a short time later.

Five days after the shooting, Aron's funeral was held at the Metro Nashville Training Academy. He was remembered as a brave dog who "acted without fear and protected his handler in the most noble fashion."

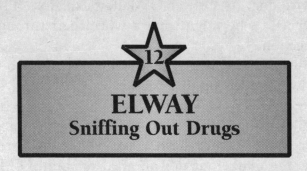

ELWAY
Sniffing Out Drugs

Dogs have an incredible sense of smell. For many years, police forces and the military have taken advantage of dogs' keen senses by using them to sniff out drugs. One dog who has proved to have a nose for this work is a golden retriever named Elway. Elway works with Kevin O'Malley, a police officer in San Francisco.

Elway tried a different career before he began his drug-sniffing work. At first, he was trained to be a service dog. Service dogs guide and assist people with a variety of disabilities. The dog attended a school for service dogs in Denver, Colorado. Because the Denver Broncos gave the school a lot of financial support, the young dog was named after the team's star quarterback, John Elway.

Unfortunately, Elway didn't have what it took to be

a service dog. As Officer O'Malley explains, "Elway's so hyper . . . he might pull a wheelchair through an intersection."

After flunking out of service-dog school, two-year-old Elway ended up at a kennel in California. That's where Officer O'Malley met his new partner. O'Malley came to the kennel to find a dog for the Drug Enforcement Agency Task Force. When he first saw Elway, the exuberant dog jumped on him. O'Malley liked Elway immediately. "I could see he'd be easy to train and fun to work with," he says.

Elway and O'Malley have worked together for six years. They usually spend part of the morning doing training exercises at a park. O'Malley will hide a drug-scented item somewhere on the grounds. Then he lets Elway off his leash and watches the dog sniff out the item. Elway's reward is nothing more than praise and a quick game with a rubber ball or a piece of rope. This may not seem like much, but it's exactly what the dog wants. When his handler rewards him in this way, Elway knows he has done his job well. "He wants to make me happy," O'Malley explains.

After the training session, O'Malley and Elway head to San Francisco Airport. O'Malley will choose a flight and ask Elway to search the bags. The team also searches storage lockers, cargo areas, and rental cars.

Elway is trained to find a number of different illegal drugs, including marijuana, cocaine, heroin, and methamphetamine. Whenever he smells something suspicious, he alerts O'Malley by scratching and biting at the package. Elway's nose is so good, he finds an average of fifteen to twenty packages a month.

Elway gets to take it easy in the afternoon. While O'Malley does paperwork in his office, the dog rests. At night, Elway goes back home for dinner and a good night's sleep.

Unlike many police dogs, Elway does not live with his handler. Instead, he lives at a kennel that has strict twenty-four-hour security. This security is necessary because drug-sniffing dogs are prime targets of smugglers and drug cartels around the world. Drug smugglers "have lost a lot of money because of the dogs," O'Malley explains. For this reason, "it's an open contract—killing dogs." A drug-sniffing dog's training also makes it incredibly valuable. These dogs can be worth more than $25,000.

In February 2001, Elway proved why drug smugglers hate him and the other drug-sniffing dogs so much. One Saturday morning at the airport, three large suitcases scheduled to be placed on a flight bound for New York were randomly screened by an X-ray machine. When the X-rays showed one bag contained nothing but a large, wrapped package, baggage inspectors became suspicious. They asked O'Malley and Elway to check out the suitcase.

As soon as he sniffed the bag, Elway scratched and bit at it. The suitcase was opened and was found to contain a large amount of marijuana wrapped in plastic. When Elway sniffed the other suitcases, he found marijuana in those too.

O'Malley noticed that another passenger had luggage just like the bags that contained the drugs. He had Elway sniff the second set of luggage. Once again, the dog alerted him to the presence of marijuana.

Police arrested the two women who owned the bags. The women confessed that there were three more women waiting in a nearby hotel with more drugs. Altogether, police found eleven bags containing $1.2 million worth of marijuana. It was the largest drug bust in San Francisco International Airport's history. And it would not have been possible without the sharp sense of smell of an exuberant retriever named Elway.

PACO
Patrolling the Border

Paco is another working dog with a nose for illegal drugs. During an assignment along the border between the United States and Mexico, this black bundle of fur found drugs in all sorts of unusual places.

Paco's handler, Lance Corporal William Abbott, is a marine. Abbott and Paco are usually stationed at the Marine Corps Air Station in Miramar, California. But in November 1999, the two were sent to El Paso, Texas, to work with the U.S. Customs Service locating drugs being smuggled into the United States.

"Several times a year, U.S. Customs solicits military support on their border crossings," explains Sergeant William Pine, who is in charge of the dog kennels at Miramar. "They have so many cars crossing every day that they just can't handle the load by themselves, so they need extra help from the military."

Abbott and Paco were stationed at the border between Texas and Mexico. Every car that comes from Mexico must stop at a checkpoint so the driver can be questioned by an inspector. Anyone who acts suspiciously or gives unusual answers to the inspector's questions is pulled out of line for a search. A computer also checks the car's license plate to see if the vehicle's owner is wanted for any crimes.

Manning a checkpoint can be a dangerous job. It's not unusual for criminals to come through the checkpoint heavily armed. One computer check led to the arrest of a man who had gunned down a narcotics agent with an AK-47 rifle.

Fortunately, Paco never faced danger from a loaded gun. However, his nose led to a lot of trouble for many drivers who came through the El Paso checkpoint. "We made three [seizures] in one day," Abbot says. "We had one bust in particular where we apprehended 416 pounds of marijuana in the trunk of a car."

Paco's nose was so keen, he set a new record for drug seizures. He had more drug busts than all the other dogs at Miramar combined, and sniffed out a total of more than 3,100 pounds of marijuana during his three-month tour of duty along the border.

Paco and Abbott have found drugs hidden almost everywhere in cars and trucks. Some vehicles have false glove compartments and floorboards where the drugs are hidden. Sometimes drugs are concealed inside door panels and gas tanks, or even inside the tires.

"I personally had a pickup truck where they raised

the bed and packed the whole bed," Abbott recalls. "Sometimes they even try to tow a vehicle across the border claiming they are taking it to be fixed, but it is loaded with marijuana. They will stop at nothing to get the drugs into the United States."

Sergeant Pine gives Paco and Abbott high praise. "He [Abbott] has a great dog, and they, as partners, have performed above and beyond expectations," Pine notes.

In recognition of the drug seizures he carried out with Paco, Abbott was nominated for a Navy and Marine Corps Achievement Medal. Meanwhile, at the end of their three-month tour of duty, the team returned to Miramar to teach a new class of dogs and handlers how to sniff out drugs at the border.

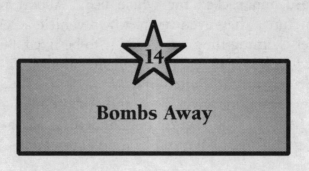

Bombs Away

Bringing a bomb or other explosives into a crowded airport or onto an airplane can cause terrible tragedy. Fortunately, there are teams who are specially trained to find explosives before they can do any damage.

There are more than 125 teams of bomb-sniffing dogs and their handlers stationed at airports all over the United States. These special K-9 dogs work for the Federal Aviation Administration, or FAA. Since 1972, their job has been to find bombs and other explosives before tragedy strikes.

The FAA's bomb-sniffing dogs are trained at Lackland Air Force Base in Texas. The handlers are police officers who volunteer for the program. The dogs, who are one or two years old when they start the program, come from special breeders and cost about $3,500 each.

Each training class lasts for twelve weeks. For the first month, the handlers work without their dogs. Instructors study the police officers carefully to see what kind of personality and working style they have. Then the instructors match each handler with a dog that has a similar personality. It is important that the teams work well together. "You don't want a hyper dog with a laid-back handler, and vice versa," says Jerry Marriott, a retired air force master sergeant and dog trainer. "Some dogs need a handler that's just as energetic and pumped up as they are or they won't work."

The most common breeds in the FAA program are Labrador retrievers, golden retrievers, and pointers. These dogs make great bomb sniffers because they are smart and friendly, and they love to work and play. The program also includes some German shepherds and Belgian Malinois. Many of these dogs were originally trained for police work, but they failed the program because they were not tough enough. "Some dogs are lovers, not fighters," explains Sergeant Marriott. "But that's the kind of dog we want. We need forgiving dogs, ones that will tolerate strangers coming up and petting them or kids teasing them, because they'll encounter crowds of people all day."

FAST FACT: Lackland trains about 350 dogs a year for many different types of military work. The dogs eat about 300 pounds of kibble a day!

By the time a dog meets its handler, it has already gone through a forty-five- to sixty-day training program of its own. First the dog must learn what explosives smell like. A trainer gives the dog a particular explosive to smell. Then he orders the dog to sit. In time, the dogs learn that anytime they smell that explosive, they should sit down to alert their handlers. Later, they learn the scents of many different explosives, such as dynamite or C-4.

Dogs are rewarded with treats and praise. "It's got to be a game for the dogs. It has to seem like playtime," says Sergeant Marriott.

FAST FACT: Bomb-sniffing dogs alert their handlers by sitting. Handlers do not want the dogs to paw at the bomb or bite it, because doing so might cause an explosion.

After the dogs learn to identify different scents, their trainers get tough. They hide the explosives in unusual or hard-to-reach places. They also mix the scents with other common smells, such as perfume or food. The dogs also learn to search in a variety of different places, including airplanes, warehouses, and offices.

Finally, it's graduation day. To graduate from the program, a dog must find at least twenty-four out of twenty-six different explosives hidden in six different places. If a dog fails this test, it goes back to school and tries again.

Bomb-sniffing dogs have proved their worth many times over, by finding hidden explosives that could have injured or killed many innocent people. Sometimes, however, these dogs do their job by not finding anything.

Officer Jim Cox of the Metropolitan Washington Airports Authority learned this firsthand. One day, a passenger on a flight to Holland did not like his seat assignment. He told the crew that he had placed a bomb on board the plane, and he would set it off unless they moved him to a different seat. The flight was delayed and all the passengers and crew got off. Then Officer Cox and his dog, a German shepherd named Yori, went to work.

Yori sniffed every inch of the plane's passenger compartment and the cargo hold. An hour later, he had found nothing. Cox declared the place was safe. "I'm very confident in Yori's abilities," he said. "If anything was in there, he would've been all over it."

As the passengers reboarded the plane, they passed Cox and Yori in the jetway. Many shook the officer's hand and thanked him. Then they applauded the officer and his dog for a job well done.

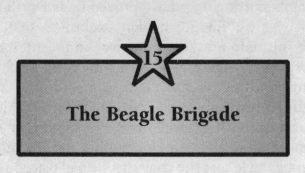

The Beagle Brigade

If you've ever flown or driven into the United States from another country, you may have met the Beagle Brigade. These beagles, wearing green vests, work in the baggage claim area of most major U.S. airports. They also patrol the borders between the United States and Canada, and the United States and Mexico. Their job is to find food and plants that are not allowed into the country.

Plants and food certainly do not sound as dangerous as bombs or drugs! However, plants, fruits, vegetables, and meat products from other countries can carry insect pests and diseases that could do serious damage to agriculture in the United States. For this reason, the United States government is determined to keep these items out.

Members of the Beagle Brigade work for the United

States Department of Agriculture's Animal and Plant Health Inspection Service (APHIS). The Beagle Brigade was started in 1984. Since then, these dogs have sniffed out thousands of pounds of illegal material every year. Today, there are more than sixty teams working in twenty-one international airports and other locations around the United States.

Beagle Brigade dogs are trained at the Department of Agriculture's National Detector Dog Training Center in Orlando, Florida. Some of the dogs come from breeders. Others are rescued from shelters or donated to the program by their owners. Beagles are used because they have a powerful sense of smell and are friendly dogs that enjoy being around lots of people.

Like bomb-sniffing and drug-sniffing dogs, members of the Beagle Brigade are taught to recognize suspicious scents. They start with strong odors, such as beef and citrus. Later, other, more subtle scents are added. When a dog smells something suspicious, it sits down and allows its handler to inspect the package and find the illegal material.

At first, the dogs and their handlers receive all their instruction at the training center. This part of the program lasts eight to twelve weeks. As a final test, the dogs are taken to Orlando Airport for a four-week tryout on the job.

As each passenger claims his or her luggage, the dogs come forward and sniff the bags. Meanwhile, the handlers ask the passenger if he or she is carrying any food or plant material. If the passenger says yes, and anything illegal is found, the handler confiscates the food. If the passenger lies about carrying illegal material, he or she can be fined up to $250.

If they pass their test at Orlando Airport, the dogs graduate from the program. They and their handlers are then assigned to another airport or facility somewhere in the United States.

Most Beagle Brigade dogs work for six to ten years. Then it's time for retirement. Usually the dog's handler adopts the beagle and keeps it as a pet. APHIS also has a list of families who want to adopt retired beagles.

FAST FACT: APHIS also runs a detector-dog program for the Department of Defense. The dogs in this program are usually Jack Russell terriers. They are stationed on the island of Guam, which has a large population of brown tree snakes. These snakes have killed many of Guam's native animals, and officials do not want the same thing to happen elsewhere. The detector dogs sniff all aircraft, vehicles, ships, and cargo to make sure no brown tree snakes are trying to hitch a ride to snake-free areas such as Hawaii or the Mariana Islands.

KAZE
From Death Row to Saving Lives

Not all hero dogs belong to the armed forces. Many civilian dogs are trained to perform search-and-rescue work (SAR, for short). SAR dogs and their handlers travel all over the United States and the world to rescue victims and find bodies. They tirelessly search buildings that have been destroyed by earthquakes, bombs, and other disasters.

Search-and-rescue dogs must be specially trained to do their job. They must learn not only how to smell and hear humans under tons of rubble, but how to work in noisy, crowded, and dangerous situations. Any breed of dog can do search-and-rescue work, as long as the animal has the right personality and dedication. German shepherds, Doberman pinschers, boxers, and Australian shepherds are commonly used, because they have the best sense of smell. Many SAR dogs are adopted from animal shelters.

Kaze was one animal-shelter dog who found a new life doing SAR work. Kaze was an Alaskan malamute who had been a sled dog in competitions. Then his owner had an accident and could no longer race. Unable to keep Kaze, she brought him to an animal shelter in Castro Valley, California. If no one adopted the five-year-old dog, he would be put to sleep.

Luckily for Kaze, a man named Daryl Lee came to the shelter and saw the dog. He realized that Kaze had what it took to be a search-and-rescue dog. After he brought Kaze home, he enrolled him in the California Rescue Dog Association's SAR training program.

Kaze passed his tests with flying colors and became one of the first Alaskan malamutes ever certified for rescue work. It did not take long for him to prove he had the right stuff.

In May 2001, on the dog's second day on the job, the sheriff's department notified Daryl Lee that a woman had gone missing. She had overdosed on prescription drugs and wandered away from home. Could Kaze and Lee find her in time?

It took only ten minutes for Kaze to locate the woman's trail. He led Lee and other rescuers to a bridge near a dam. Without pausing, Kaze ran under the bridge and found the missing woman.

The victim was rushed to the hospital. She was in a coma, and doctors later said that she would have been dead in less than an hour if Kaze had not found her. The woman made a full recovery. And Kaze had begun an exciting new career.

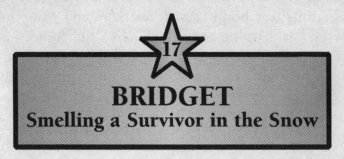

BRIDGET
Smelling a Survivor in the Snow

It was a stormy day in Alpine Meadows, a ski area in California's Sierra Mountains. Snow had been falling for several days. Authorities were worried about avalanches. An avalanche is a large mass of snow and ice that travels quickly down a mountain, burying everything in its path.

Anna Conrad worked as a ski-lift operator at Alpine Meadows. Despite the danger, she came to work that afternoon. She was changing in the locker room when she heard a roar. A huge avalanche had started at the top of the mountain. Within seconds, giant slabs of snow and ice had buried everything in sight. The force of the avalanche was so strong that buildings exploded.

Conrad was knocked unconscious by the avalanche. When she woke up, she realized that a row of lockers had fallen across a bench. She was trapped in the tiny space underneath the lockers, 15 feet under the snow.

Within two hours, rescue workers and equipment arrived at Alpine Meadows by helicopter and snowmobile. The rescue team included two search-and-rescue dogs and their handlers. The dogs quickly began searching the disaster site, which covered five acres of the snowy mountain. Although they found lots of equipment and some bodies, they did not find any survivors.

As workers and dogs searched high above her, Conrad managed to dress herself in clothing from the lockers to keep warm. She ate snow. And she waited.

Rescue efforts went on for several days. But the bad weather made things difficult. The rescue workers had to stop several times because of blizzards and the danger of more avalanches.

Three days after the disaster, a German shepherd named Bridget stopped above the spot where Conrad was buried. She had smelled the trapped woman through the snow. Bridget alerted her handler, Roberta Huber. Huber called to Conrad, and Conrad yelled back. She thought she was about to be rescued. But Huber could not hear Conrad's voice. Soon after, another snowstorm hit the mountain. Rescue work had to stop for two days.

As soon as the weather cleared, Bridget and Huber came back. Huber was concerned that Bridget would not be able to find Conrad's scent again, because so many other rescue workers had been over the area. Would Conrad's scent be lost in the other smells?

Huber need not have worried. Bridget went right to the location where Conrad was buried. She whined and pawed at the snow.

Rescue workers rushed to the spot with chain saws and shovels. They dug a tunnel into the snow and lowered Bridget into it. Bridget pointed in the direction they should go, and the workers kept digging.

Finally workers reached Conrad. It had been five days since the avalanche buried the young woman. To everyone's amazement, she was alive and conscious. Bridget licked Conrad's face as the woman was rushed to the hospital.

Seven people were killed in the avalanche at Alpine Meadows. But Anna Conrad survived because of Bridget's terrific sense of smell. One of the happiest moments of Conrad's recovery occurred when she received two very special visitors at the hospital: Roberta Huber and Bridget.

FAST FACT: The first search-and-rescue dogs were Saint Bernards who rescued lost travelers in the Swiss Alps hundreds of years ago.

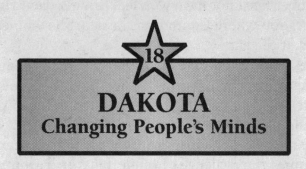

18

DAKOTA
Changing People's Minds

Many people hear the words "pit bull" and picture a vicious dog that attacks for no reason. Pit bulls got this bad reputation because they are frequently owned by cruel and irresponsible humans who train them as attack dogs to protect drug dealers and other criminals, or use them in illegal dog-fighting rings. Other pit bull owners do not train them at all and allow them to run loose and get into trouble. In recent years, many people who have never even met a pit bull have come to fear them because they have heard horror stories about these dogs on TV or in newspapers. Animal shelters around the country are filled with pit bulls who are likely to be destroyed simply because potential owners are afraid to adopt them.

The truth is, a pit bull is no more dangerous than any other breed of dog. Any dog will learn to be mean in the hands of a cruel owner. Pit bulls who are used for fighting or as attack dogs have been trained to behave this way. If a pit bull is raised in a loving home, he or she can be a safe and wonderful pet. And some pit bulls can be much, much more.

Kristine Crawford is a longtime search-and-rescue worker from California. She works with her beloved dogs, Cheyenne and Dakota. Both are pit bulls.

Crawford rescued Cheyenne when the dog was a sickly puppy who was about to be destroyed just because she was a pit bull. Crawford trained Cheyenne in obedience work and tracking, which teaches a dog to follow a scent. They eventually became a SAR team.

Not long after Cheyenne became a SAR dog, she and Crawford went to see a litter of pit bull puppies. Cheyenne became very attached to one puppy and kept carrying her to Crawford's car. The breeder offered to let Crawford take the puppy. That's how Dakota joined the family. A few weeks later, Crawford found out that Dakota's breeder had been arrested for running a dog-fighting ring. All the other puppies had been destroyed. Dakota escaped this fate and became a search-and-rescue dog like Cheyenne.

Crawford and Dakota have been involved in many searches. In one of their most memorable adventures, Dakota ended up saving her handler!

Early one morning, Crawford's search-and-rescue pager went off with an urgent call. A young man had gone hiking in the California mountains and had never come home. Crawford and Dakota gathered their equipment and headed out into the wilderness, along with several other SAR teams.

At the search site, the pair made their way along a narrow deer trail on the edge of a steep ravine. Looking down, Crawford saw jagged rocks hundreds of feet below them. One wrong step, and she and Dakota could plunge over the edge to their deaths.

Dakota was busy sniffing the air, searching for any scent of the missing man. As Crawford walked close to the ravine, she suddenly heard a terrifying sound. An animal was growling in the bushes only a short distance away. Crawford remembered that mountain lions had been seen in the area. When the growling became louder, she decided it was time to get away. But the only escape was along the narrow deer trail, which was slippery from a recent rain.

Crawford concluded that a slippery trail was better than a ferocious mountain lion. She and Dakota made their way carefully through the mud, Crawford holding tightly to bushes as she walked along the edge of the ravine. Suddenly the wet rocks moved and the path gave way under her feet. Crawford slipped and fell about 50 feet into the ravine. Dakota, who was working off-leash, remained on the trail.

Luckily, Crawford was not hurt in the fall. But how was she going to get out of the deep ravine? The sides were too steep and wet for her to climb out. She grabbed her radio to call for help, but the radio had been smashed in the fall. Crawford yelled for help, but the strong wind carried her words away. She was stuck.

Then she remembered the mountain lion she had heard in the bushes. *I hope the mountain lion isn't stupid enough to come down into this ravine the way I did,* she thought. Just to make sure, Crawford looked up. There was Dakota, peering over the edge. The dog started to scramble down to her partner, but Crawford quickly yelled, "Stay!" She didn't want Dakota to get stuck too.

Suddenly Crawford had an idea. She tied her broken radio to the end of a rope she was carrying. Then she swung the rope and threw it up over the side to Dakota. "Pick it up!" Crawford called to the dog.

Dakota loved to play tug, so she wasted no time grabbing the rope in her mouth. With Dakota pulling hard on the other end, Crawford was able to use the rope to pull herself out of the ravine. Then she and Dakota rejoined the search, as if nothing had happened. It was all in a day's work for the team! Later, there was more good news. The missing young man was found alive, trapped on a ledge, and was rescued by a helicopter.

Crawford and her dogs have also trained to do pet therapy. During visits to nursing homes and hospitals, Cheyenne and Dakota give unconditional love and comfort to people who are in pain or who suffer from loneliness. Crawford says, "Cheyenne and Dakota search for 'lost souls' with the same commitment with which they search for lost beings. Watching them bring the life back into the eyes of a sick or dying person, if even for a moment, makes all the work worth the effort."

Crawford is determined to show the world that pit bulls are terrific dogs. "When my search pager goes off, my dogs are waiting at the door, ready to find a lost person, to save a life, or to bring closure to a family by finding their deceased loved one. My pit bulls do not know that people are biased, that people do not like them, that they have to work harder than everyone else to earn their spot, or that some people may actually try to hurt them out of fear or ignorance. All they know, deep in their hearts, is that they have work to do. They are always ready to do it regardless of weather, time, or obstacle . . . and they will not quit."

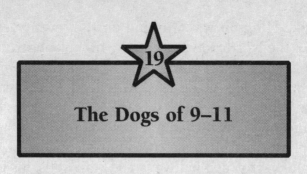

The Dogs of 9–11

September 11, 2001, was a day that changed America forever. At 8:46 that morning, a plane that had been hijacked by terrorists crashed into the North Tower of the World Trade Center in New York City. Seventeen minutes later, another hijacked plane struck the South Tower. Both towers erupted in flames. Less than ninety minutes later, they collapsed, killing thousands of civilians, firefighters, police officers, and other rescue workers.

As the towers burned and fell, additional rescue workers rushed to the scene to try to find survivors in the rubble. Amazingly, although almost three thousand lives were lost that day, thousands more people were saved. Two of the lucky ones were blind men who were led out of the wreckage by their faithful guide dogs.

ROZELLE

Mike Hingson was working on the seventy-eighth floor of the North Tower when the first plane struck the building a few floors above him. Hingson had company in his office. His guide dog, Rozelle, a three-year-old yellow Labrador retriever, was sleeping under his desk.

Hingson knew he had to escape, but because he had been blind since birth, he could not see where to go. In the smoky, crowded hallways and stairwells, his other, usually sharp senses were of little help. That's where Rozelle came in. The dog led Hingson down seventy-eight flights of stairs. It took a long time, but Hingson and Rozelle reached the ground floor and safety. Outside the building, a coworker told Hingson that both towers were on fire and he had better get out of the area. As the man and his dog ran away, they heard the South Tower collapsing behind them.

Hingson had nothing but praise for his faithful companion. "She never hesitated," he said. "She never panicked."

DORADO

Rozelle was not the only guide dog at the World Trade Center that day. Omar Eduardo Rivera was working on the seventieth floor of the North Tower when the first plane hit. Being unable to see, Rivera could not imagine how he could get out of the building, so he decided to stay in his office. But he did not want his guide dog, Dorado, to be trapped with him. So he took off the dog's leash and commanded him to leave.

Dorado started to go down the stairs alone. But when he realized that Rivera was not following him, he stopped and went back to the blind man's side. For the first time, he refused to do what Rivera told him. He would not leave. Finally, Rivera put Dorado's leash back on and let him lead the way down the stairs.

Rivera and Dorado joined hundreds of people trying to escape. "Everywhere there was a sense of terror," Rivera later said. The air was full of smoke and heat and broken glass. But Dorado did not panic.

Once again, Rivera decided that he could never make it to safety. "I thought I was lost forever—the noise and the heat were terrifying—but I had to give Dorado the chance of escape," he explained. "So I unclipped his lead, ruffled his head, gave him a nudge, and ordered Dorado to go. I hoped he would be able to quickly run down the stairs without me and get to safety."

For a moment, Dorado was swept away by the crush of people hurrying down the stairs. Then something unexpected happened. The dog turned around and went back. When Rivera felt his familiar furry head against his leg, he knew what he had to do.

Rivera grabbed hold of his dog and let the animal lead him down the stairs and into the safety of the streets below. The hour-long journey was the most difficult walk of Rivera's life, but he made it with Dorado at his side.

"It was then that I knew for certain he loved me just as much as I loved him," Rivera said of his dog. "He was prepared to die in the hope he might save my life. I owe my life to Dorado—my companion and best friend."

RICKY

Most search-and-rescue dogs are large breeds, such as German shepherds or Labrador retrievers. Then there's Ricky the rat terrier. This two-year-old dog is only 17 inches long and weighs less than 18 pounds. He's the smallest SAR dog in the United States. But there's nothing small about the job Ricky did at the World Trade Center.

Ricky arrived at Ground Zero (the site of the World Trade Center collapse) from Seattle, Washington, along with his partner, firefighter Janet Linker. The two spent ten days searching through the rubble and successfully located several bodies. Whenever Ricky found a body, he signaled Linker by staying very still and staring at her, with the fur on his body standing straight up.

Ricky's small size helped him squeeze into holes and gaps between the steel beams that were too tiny for other dogs to even think about crawling into. Ricky had also been trained to climb ladders—something larger dogs cannot usually do. His excellent climbing ability helped him navigate the towering piles of rubble at the scene.

Ricky had been doing search-and-rescue work for only about a year, so sometimes he worked with a larger and more experienced golden retriever named Thunder. Ricky would crawl into holes where Thunder could not fit. Whenever Ricky found a body, Thunder would confirm his finds by lying down at the spot to signal his human partner, Kent Olson. Then rescue workers would come to the spot to remove the body.

After almost two weeks at Ground Zero, Linker and Ricky returned to Seattle. A month later, the Seattle City Council held a special ceremony to honor the people who had helped at the World Trade Center. Four SAR dogs, including Ricky, were also invited to participate. As the little dog sat on the podium, wearing his official SAR uniform, he warmed the hearts of everyone at the ceremony.

CODY

Sometimes rescuers get into trouble and need some canine assistance to get out. That's just what happened to Paul Morgan, who came to Ground Zero with his SAR dog, Cody. Like other rescuers, Morgan and Cody hoped to find survivors trapped in the rubble of the Twin Towers. Sadly, all they found were bodies. But they knew that finding the victims' remains was important too, so they continued to work tirelessly.

At one point, Morgan and Cody were searching the rubble 10 feet underneath a fire truck that had been destroyed in the collapse. Morgan and Cody crawled into the hole. Morgan could not see anything, but suddenly Cody began to whimper and scratch at the ground. "We have a body down here!" Morgan called up to firefighters above him. He and his dog climbed out to allow the firefighters into the hole to locate the body of one of their fallen comrades.

Cody found three more bodies in the next thirty minutes. Then something terrifying happened. Morgan became trapped under a slab of concrete! His boots had gotten caught in between some chunks of concrete, and he could not crawl backward out of the hole. To make matters worse, the area was completely dark. Morgan had no idea how to get out.

Morgan might have panicked, but Cody did not. Instead, the dog turned Morgan toward the left and began to pull him. Morgan managed to free his feet. Then he grabbed the dog's leash and let the dog find the way out. Finally the two of them crawled out of the hole and were lifted to safety by some firefighters.

Cody was exhausted, filthy, and thirsty after working so hard. Morgan found a metal tray in the trash, but he did not have any water to fill it. Suddenly a line of firefighters stepped forward and began pouring water from their own bottles into the tray for Cody to drink. It was their way of saying "Thank you."

SERVUS

People were not the only ones injured during the rescue and recovery work at Ground Zero. The dogs were also in danger. Fires burned underneath the rubble in many places. This meant the ground and the steel beams were often hot enough to burn the dogs' feet. Smoke and dust filled the air and made it hard to breathe. The dogs had to walk on jagged pieces of concrete, broken glass, and shattered steel. Often, the piles of rubble shifted dangerously under the dogs' feet. This movement could cause falls and broken bones.

Teams of veterinarians were at the scene to care for the dogs. They treated as many as one hundred dogs a day. Most of the injuries were cut or burned paws.

To protect the dogs, the New York City Police Department made an urgent request for "booties," which are special waterproof socks with padded soles. Several companies donated hundreds of these booties to the rescue effort. "Those dogs put their lives on the line for the people they're trying to rescue," said a spokeswoman for one dog-supply company. "They're no different from police- and firemen. They need protective gear too."

Sometimes even protective gear could not keep the dogs from being injured. On September 13, Chris Christensen and his Belgian Malinois, Servus, were climbing a pile of twisted steel, concrete, and glass. The two had come to Ground Zero from East Carondelet, Illinois, where they worked for the police department. Servus was in the lead. Suddenly he slipped and fell 20 feet down what had once been an escalator. The dog landed face-first in a thick pile of ash and dust.

Christensen rushed to his dog's side. At first he thought Servus had broken his leg. Then he realized that the dog had inhaled so much ash, he could not breathe.

Christensen raced to help his dog. He flung Servus's 70-pound body over his shoulder and ran, screaming, "I need help!" A dozen firefighters, police officers, and medical personnel were at his side in an instant. A nurse inserted an IV into the dog, while a firefighter began suctioning the debris from Servus's nose and mouth. Servus had gone into convulsions from lack of air by the time a police car raced him to a nearby medical center.

Fortunately, a team of five veterinarians was able to save Servus's life. He was ready to leave the hospital just a few hours later. Christensen was happy to make such an effort to help his dog. Servus had saved his life twice during their partnership. "I just couldn't let him die," he said.

SIRIUS

Only one dog was killed during the World Trade Center disaster and the recovery efforts that followed. Sirius, a bomb-sniffing Labrador retriever who was part of the Port Authority Police Department's K-9 unit, was trapped in the department's basement offices in the World Trade Center and died when the buildings collapsed.

When the first plane hit the building, Sirius's handler, Officer David Lim, had rushed upstairs to see what was happening. He wanted to find out what the situation was before he took Sirius with him. Unfortunately, Officer Lim was unable to return for his dog before the buildings collapsed.

Officer Lim did not escape the World Trade Center unharmed. In the collapse, he was buried in a stairway and had to be rescued. Officer Lim recovered and went on to train a new canine partner to carry on Sirius's important work.

On January 22, 2002, Sirius's remains were found at Ground Zero. Like all the heroes of 9–11, he received full police honors as his body was carried from the site.

HEALING WOUNDED HEARTS

Although most of the dogs who helped in the days following the World Trade Center disaster were police dogs or search-and-rescue dogs, there were others who had a different job to do. Specially trained therapy dogs also stepped in to help victims of the disaster, their families, and the rescue workers.

Therapy dogs are trained to bring comfort and good cheer to people in hospitals, nursing homes, and other treatment facilities. Therapy dogs can be any breed, or mixed-breed dogs. The important thing is that they are gentle, warm-hearted, and able to give love to people in stressful situations. Other animals also do therapy work, including cats, rabbits, and birds, but dogs are the most common.

In the days after the World Trade Center collapse, teams of therapy dogs and their handlers arrived at an assistance center where victims and their families had come to find help. As people waited in line or tried to wade through the mountains of paperwork, the dogs were there to comfort them and even make them smile.

Other dogs visited police and fire stations near Ground Zero to comfort rescue workers. Somehow, people felt a little better after they played with a dog, or just buried their face in its fur and gave it a big hug. "This is the most rewarding thing I've ever done," said one handler.

Usually, the dogs waited for people to approach them. Sometimes, however, the dogs went directly to people who needed them. One handler described how her dog, Fidel, walked over to a crying woman who had lost her job because of the disaster. The woman picked up the dog and exclaimed, "He really felt my pain."

Doing therapy work is rewarding, but it is also hard on the dogs. Because they are in stressful, emotion-filled situations, the dogs work for only two hours a day, a few days a week. Many handlers report that their dogs are exhausted after comforting so many people. Still, the dogs and their handlers wouldn't have it any other way.

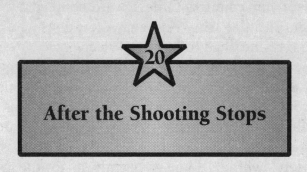

After the Shooting Stops

What happens to war dogs, police dogs, and search-and-rescue dogs when they can no longer serve? Police dogs and search-and-rescue dogs usually remain with their handlers as family pets. The fate of war dogs has been quite different, however.

Most of the dogs who served with the U.S. Army, Marines, and Coast Guard during World War II were returned to their owners at the end of the war. After months or years in the armed services, though, dogs could not just go back to civilian life. They had to be retrained to get along with people and not attack strangers. The military certainly did not want war dogs injuring or even killing innocent civilians!

Dogs who were successfully retrained were returned to their owners with an honorable discharge and a certificate describing the canine's faithful service to his or her country. Others were adopted by their handlers or other army veterans. A few dogs who could not be retrained had to be put to sleep.

During the Vietnam War, the military changed its policy about war dogs. Up until then, the animals had been considered soldiers. But in Vietnam, the dogs were classified as equipment. When American forces withdrew from Vietnam in 1975, almost all the dogs were left behind. Some were given to the South Vietnamese army, but their handlers did not work well with the dogs. Other dogs were abandoned, and many of these animals were killed or died of starvation.

The military did try to return some dogs to the United States. Many of the dogs had become sick in Vietnam, however, and officials worried that bringing war dogs home would introduce new diseases into the United States. For a while, the military isolated hundreds of dogs in an effort to see which of them were healthy enough to be sent home. But the fear of disease was so great that only 204 of the more than 4,000 dogs who served in Vietnam were shipped back to the United States before the program ended.

Even the dogs who did return to the United States were not released from military service. The military had spent thousands of dollars to purchase and train war dogs, and they were reluctant to let this huge financial investment go to waste. So war dogs continued to serve. They protected the president and other important government leaders, patrolled military institutions, or sniffed out drugs, explosives, and other materials at airports and along the United States' borders with Canada and Mexico. When the dogs became too old or sick to work, they were put to sleep.

Recently, veterans who worked with war dogs have been pressuring the military and the United States government to allow the dogs to be released to their handlers when the animals can no longer work. In June 2000, an eight-year-old Belgian Malinois named Robby was sent to Lackland Air Force Base because he was suffering from arthritis. Doctors at the base examined Robby and decided that he was so sick, he would have to be put to sleep. Robby's handler found out about this decision and begged the military to let him care for the dog for the rest of the animal's life.

When the air force refused, Robby's handler told his story to the media. Thousands of American citizens e-mailed and wrote to the Department of Defense. They also contacted their representatives in Congress. A bill requiring the military to find other alternatives to destroying sick and aging war dogs easily passed in the House of Representatives and the Senate. President Bill Clinton signed the bill into law on November 6, 2000.

Unfortunately, the bill could not help Robby. His medical condition became so bad during that winter that he had to be put to sleep in January 2001. However, since Robby's death, a few war dogs have been returned to their handlers or other qualified caretakers. As for Robby, on June 24, 2001, he was buried at Hartsdale Pet Cemetery in Hartsdale, New York, in an official ceremony.

Honoring Heroic Dogs

When Robby was buried, his remains were placed at the base of a war dog monument at Hartsdale Pet Cemetery. This monument was built in 1918 and was the first war dog memorial in the nation. Every year a special ceremony at Hartsdale honors the thousands of war dogs who have died in military service.

The United States has only a few monuments honoring war dogs. In 1994, a memorial to heroic war dogs was unveiled at a naval station in Guam, an island in the Pacific belonging to the United States, where twenty-five war dogs are buried. Their names are written on a granite monument topped by a life-size sculpture of a Doberman pinscher, along with the words "Always Faithful."

In 1999, the War Dog Memorial Fund was started.

In February of 2000, about one hundred veterans and their dogs gathered in Riverside, California, to dedicate a memorial near the March Field Air Museum. This monument features an 18-foot statue of a German shepherd and his handler. Underneath the statue are these words: "They Protected Us on the Field of Battle. They Watch Over Our Eternal Rest. We Are Grateful." In October 2000, an identical monument was unveiled at the Fort Benning Infantry Museum in Fort Benning, Georgia.

The War Dog Memorial Fund is seeking greater recognition for our country's canine heroes. Its members have been petitioning the U.S. Postal Service to issue a stamp honoring the dogs. They have also asked for permission to plant a tree at Arlington National Cemetery in Virginia, the place where many of America's greatest military heroes and government leaders are laid to rest, but so far they have not been allowed to do so.

Meanwhile, many dog handlers have created their own memorials to the dogs who served with them. These veterans have set up websites to tell their stories and express their deep love for their dogs. Others remember their dogs through personal collections of photographs, scrapbooks, and their own memories.

Over the past few years, the American people have learned more about the heroic dogs who served our country. Maybe one day—one day soon—our nation will officially thank these canine heroes.

FOR MORE INFORMATION

There are many books on war dogs, search-and-rescue dogs, and police dogs. Check your local library or bookstore.

The following websites are also a great source of information on these canine heroes:

The American Legion Post 127 War Dog Memorial
http://www.eagleid.com/post127/dogs.htm
This website contains a list of many war dogs, along with some stories of their deeds.

The Beagle Brigade
http://www.aphis.usda.gov/ppq
This website has more information about the Beagle Brigade and other government detector-dog programs.

Dogs in the News
http://dogsinthenews.com
Click on this website for news stories and photos about brave and interesting dogs.

The Dogs of the World Trade Center
http://www.dogspeak.ca/WTCDogs.htm
This photo essay honors some of the rescue dogs who helped in the recovery effort at Ground Zero.

Fallen K-9 Memorials
http://members.dandy.net/~lulu/memorial.html
http://members.dandy.net/~lulu/k92001
mem-index.html
These web pages include photos and stories of police dogs killed in the line of duty.

MWDs—Lackland Air Force Base 341st Training Squadron
http://www.lackland.af.mil/341trs
Check out this website for the history of Lackland's dog-training program, as well as specific details about how the dogs are trained for military work.

For Pits' Sake
http://www.forpitssake.org
This website features Kristine Crawford and her search-and-rescue dogs Cheyenne and Dakota.

Scout Dog Pages
http://www.scoutdogpages.com
This website includes many stories of dogs and handlers who served in the Vietnam War, including Wolf and Charlie Cargo.

Valor—Police K-9 Officers and Dogs Killed in Service
http://www.policek9.com/Valor/valor.html
This memorial site for police dogs includes stories, photos, and remembrances.

The Vietnam Dog Handler Association
http://www.vdhaonline.org
Check out this website for information on the National War Dog Memorial Fund, as well as general information about war dogs who served in Vietnam.

War Dogs Bibliography
http://www.qmfound.com/War_Dogs_ Bibliography.htm
This is a thorough list of books and magazine articles about dogs who have served in all branches of the military.

Working Dogs Websites
http://www.doginformat.com
This website includes links to many police, K-9, military, and government dog web pages and articles.

You can also write to the National War Dog Memorial Fund at:

> National War Dog Memorial Fund
> c/o Vietnam Dog Handler Association
> PO Box 5658, Dept. P
> Oceanside, CA 92052-5658